THE UTERUS IS AN IMPOSSIBLE FOREST

Shannon Kearns

RAW DOG SCREAMING PRESS

The Uterus is an Impossible Forest © 2025 by Shannon Kearns

Published by Raw Dog Screaming Press
Bowie, MD

First Edition

Cover art copyright 2025 by Shannon Kearns
Cover design and book layout by Jennifer Barnes

Printed in the United States of America

ISBN: 978-1-947879-98-0
Library of Congress Control Number:
2025942883

RawDogScreaming.com

For my children, forever

Contents

Author's Note 7
The Uterus is an Impossible Forest 11

PART ONE: Spiral 13
Three Mothers 14
Harbingers 18
Astrologer 20
Woman as Bone 22
Dream with Monolith 23
Pieces of a woman's body 25
Nervous Breakdown 27
Cave of Eggs 28
Thing Apart 31
Death in XIII Parts 32
Origin 35

PART TWO: Poisoned Apple 37
Magdalene 38
Prayer for a Witch 41
Night Out 42
Yellow 44
Lotus Eater 46
My Body is a Church 48
The Burning 49
Lilith 51
Body, Undone 53

Dream Inside of a Glass House 54
Mad Woman 55
Woman as Yes 57
Woman as Artificial [Intelligence] 59
Skin 60

PART THREE: Mother Wolf 63
Habits 64
Postpartum 66
Broken Waters 67
Alchemical Reaction 68
When my body bleeds, I dream of spirals 69
Domestic Silence 70
Hornet's Nest 73
i dream my body splits in two 74
Nine Months 75
My breasts leak soft tears 77
Mastitis 78
House 79
Waxing Moon 80
i dream my body is a grave 81
i bleed red dreams 82
Visitations 83
Sea-Hag 87

PART FOUR: Return 89
Protection 90
Hecate 91
White Gardenias 93
Once again, I find myself on the other side of my tomb 94
Pyre 95

Scarecrow	96
Door	97
Sister-Self	98
Rebirth	99
Love Letter to a Witch	100
Crow	101
Orchid	102
Spun	103
Hair	104
Return	105
Holding my child for the first time	107
Previously Published	108

Author's Note

The Uterus is an Impossible Forest is a compilation of poems drawing upon themes of motherhood, witchcraft, feminine power, and desire. These poems form a bridge between speculative and horror poetry, dancing between shades of darkness to capture the magic and mystery inherent in its layers. Inspired by myths, fairy tales, and legends, this work seeks to subvert patriarchal themes, calling forth the power of the feminine through a dissection of what it means to be in a queer, female body while mothering young children. The poems in *The Uterus is an Impossible Forest* move through a journey of disintegration of a former self into a reintegration of a new self that embodies the power and potency of the archetypal witch.

I am terrified by this dark thing

That sleeps in me;

All day I feel its soft, feathery turnings, its malignity

>—Sylvia Plath, "Elm"

The Uterus is an Impossible Forest

and in the center

    is a wolf.

She has not been invited,

    but she has become comfortable.

In the den of a barren

    tree, she waits. She has been waiting

a long time. There is a child

    in the forest. She can smell

its laughter rocking

    like a cradle. *It has passed*

this way. Moon-time yanks

    her open, licking air, licking

bark, licking strangled

    need, tight as a tumor,

heavy as bleeding time. She wants

    the child to hear her

and come running. She wants the child

    to forget she exists.

Easier that way.

    She has counted

the years one by

    one, etched the passing

of time in ruined hieroglyphs

    on her bedroom wall. Sanctuary.

She has forgotten: she is never

    safe. She has for-

gotten: this is not a place where

    she gets to choose.

PART ONE
SPIRAL

It's easy to get lost in the woods.
Even if you set off on a straight path,
you will start to curve and inevitably
end up walking in a circle.
—Erin E. Adams

Three Mothers

After Sylvia Plath's "Three Women"

> *I am the center of an atrocity.*
> *What pains, what sorrows must I be mothering?*

Great-Grandmother:

I am a river, a bleeding
yawn. My lips form an O–

oval cave of slippery
eels. They swim,

swim and multiply just
by thinking about their

eyes. They eat light.
They are nibbling me

at the stem. I cannot speak
of their blankness, only

they press my abdomen
like an orchid blossom

slipped between
the pages of a thick

book shut tight.
I feel wrung

through the middle,
twisted into the shape

of a distant cave, a home
for their silence

as the red night
of a dying sun

sharpens a cold stave
in the corner of my eye.

Grandmother:

I am swollen with a third
child and nothing is okay.

I dreamt the child changed
into a cotton doll

filling me with dry
white filaments, its eyes

two fists tightened against

the breaking. Its stuffing

poking through loose seams
as I tried to repair them, one

by one. No one has forewarned
me, no one has spoken–

only in dreams do I know
something is wrong.

And the mouse at my doorstep,
dead prune, its tongue lolled

in pre-decay stiffness
whispers: *you, next*

Mother:

This is my reckoning—
you've found me at
the end. No one lives
in this cave but me

and a wolf. I have
searched for the shiny

thing with warm eyes
and a full breast–

found nothing
but my mouth wrapped

around a cigarette, a can
of beer, a man. Who

has the right to question
where I find love when

love has always been a fire
and I a moth, hungry

for its heat. Now you want
to know why I've hidden

a child inside of me
and she's drowning?

Harbingers

say forever and I'll show you a child who is not a child

    but a word shrill as a hawk's cry, haunted

by her potential eternities: a body

    taken from another body bloodied and offered

to one found barren. mother, did you look to the sky for a sign

    that you should bear me? did you find patterns

in the stars or wonder at the torpid swing of a pendulum

    or open a bible to the word *yes* written in a corner

of your permission? maybe I'm only here because

    of harbingers: an egg dropped in a pit

of boiling water bearing a slick, yellow smile,

    a handful of runes tossed like dead

leaves, or a dream–the kind that moves

  in waves, or a song that came

on in the drugstore while you thumbed

  the paper comfort of dollar bills then waited for the smoke

to rise. i know that smell of acrid loss [it's mine too].

  say forever and I'll show you a child who has hidden

her eternities in her breast pocket. sometimes,

  she shuffles them like a deck of cards then lets them fall

where they may. a chance, a reversal, a risk. a queen

  of cups, a mother–say forever

and I'll show you a child

watching the sky for a sign

Astrologer

Tell me I'm not born
under a house of speckled fate,
my stars an attack of tossed glitter,
impossible to scrape into proper placements.

Tell me my divinity is not cast
despicably in soggy tea leaf
dregs or shuffled into an undulating
fortune. My body snuck

in through the side door
of an unwed (unknown) mother,
our synastry a confused constellation
sunk in a bed of descension.

Her fate my fault lines
drawn in an oval, a black
cavity in my eleventh house
of belonging, my fifth house
of nurturing (paintings & children

& cakes). Tell me my moon
does not cling listlessly to
her retrograde and my exaltation

of Jupiter does not perch tragically
in the cracked amphitheater of a
broken mythology. Tell me I can

dance lightly under Scorpio's
pregnant welter then whisper
these magic words to me:

Uterus/Umbilicus/Placenta/Orphan

Woman as Bone

(for my mother)

    Mother, even as I write this, you are shrinking.
    Once, you loomed like a willow. I'd turn
    to your body, body that was never my home.
    Now, there is less. Perhaps your skeleton
    grows tired of bearing so much loss: surrender
    to a dream–feel your body morph into mother,
    your breasts full, your narrow hips a wide furnace.

    Perhaps your body is a hungry, hollow-boned
    bird preparing for flight, swallowing its own marrow.
    Perhaps your crumpling is not a frailty but an invitation:

    what are bones but another hard fact to face?

Dream with Monolith

I. Fog

There is a road covered with snow surrounded by mountains. I know

they exist, even though I cannot see them. We are driving

in a car toward nothing. Mother, you have led me here, this dead-

end, a road masked in fog. I say *go no further*. You

say *let's try*. The expanse so white, so thick and knowing.

It breathes deeply generating oxygen and strife,

a meditation on erosion of hope. No hand can pass through

such a choke. I turn around–there is nothing for me. Nothing

but a mystery, potent and closed.

II. Monolith

Obsidian and granite, a bubble of stone, massive and smooth, a warm breast, curved hip balanced by a thin

    neck, black swan letter S for *swell*. We cling

to her, so small in her rock arms, face etched

    with a knife, smile knowing, becalmed, omniscient.

Mother of my dreams, you point the way, your nose an arrow

    away from the fog toward the mountains, crystalline and quantum,

pulling each tendril of hurt tenderly from my budding decline.

Pieces of a woman's body

Alone,
alone and unmade

you've planted my bones,
my pieces yielding to your dank

summations, alone and alone
I tell you,

don't take this lightly,
my hollow essence,

my held tongue,
brittle kaleidoscope

gems, dust over dust over
dust collected in your cupped

hands, gripping
a fragile neck and bird

bones and pointed corners.
I tell you, these corners

are my spell.
I tell you, my body

is my spell.
Believe me when

I say:
I lay prone in a cold bath,

lights flickering, my skin the shape
of melon rind and smooth breezes,

tender labyrinth, blistering cry of
fruit-sweetness a part,

apart—

Nervous Breakdown

For my grandmother

Tell me, did you suffer the rose, knotted and frail in your thin hands? Was all your kneeling for naught? Did you execute small vices and pile them, tipping, in your medicine cabinet? I know I shouldn't ask, but [was this caused by] the doctors' tone [or] your torn birthing gown [or] your wooden bed with the cross always watching? Did you hold a glass child and fear it would break? Perhaps you wrote letters to Eve and warned her against screaming. Perhaps those letters were found by God and that's why they sent you away. I've written letters, myself, not to Eve but to a crow. Am I like you? My windows are dull with fog and residue. My mouth is a tempest.

When you died, I stood in a church, my belly filled with a son. They paraded your quiet urn down a long column of dissonance. There was silence and flowers. Someone spoke of heaven. I have to—no, I have to know—[was this caused by] no one spoke, of course, no one spoke of your sadnesses. I know I shouldn't ask but were they yours, yours alone?

Cave of Eggs

Once, I was a guest at a seance

    or, I was a guest

in someone else's dream. Unclear. There was a table

    and a candle on a brass throne melting wax

into ivory rivers. Nothing in this room

    was made of glass, therefore

nothing in this room was easily

    broken. Every word became an echo

of the one before. Every word became

    a mother, their bodies

cupping each other like Russian dolls, faces

    both known and unknown, shadowed like bats'

eyes peering through translucent wings. I wanted to touch

    their cheeks, some sallow and creased

with navigable lines, others scarred like peeling tree

    bark. One was alabaster white and

eyeless, one could only squint as if it were all

    too much. Another lay in a childbirth

bed, blood running in thirsty rivers,

    her arms spread like wings, her voice

a whisper: was her daughter

    playing in the forest, had she found

the wolf in the center of everything? One knelt

    before me as if I were the God she had been praying

for, clasped my hands while another

    language spilled from her split tongue–

all I could hear was a hiss.

    I wanted to press

each of their faces against my own,

    scream into their open mouths:

where have you been hiding and

    can you take me with you?

Thing Apart

Here I am: a gospel
of deceased notions,
each tick of a clock's
hand spreading time

like dandelion seeds,
yellow and indignant.
I am set like a silhouette
against laughter: a brilliant,
dying symphony. Hear

the tender placements
of each note, a voice
soft and separate calling
mother. None of my

words can be cradled.
Here I am: a piece of
misplaced china, rubbed
clean and set aside only
to collect ashes in my cave.

Death in XIII Parts

After Wallace Stevens' "Thirteen Ways of Looking at a Blackbird"

I.
You have found yourself dead again & again,
fall's death-wish blooms steady on your cheeks.

II.
The earth is a patient witness,
of your wandering winter, the toll
of a white funeral.

III.
How many times must you
press your stiff chest to frozen ground to stop
your heart from beating?

IV.
I watch you bury yourself
in cold mist, blank girl hiding
in a wooden coffin.

V.
Your box was paraded
like a victory for men.
I am sick with your silence.

VI.
Whispered vespers,
you dangle a prayer
from your gray tongue.

VII.
Your body is licked
clean by the mouth
of a raging fire.

VIII.
What remains of your time
but a memory of picking
bleeding hearts and crushing
their pulp between your fingers?

IX.
What remains after the flame
but a swath of dust
flickering in sunlight
beneath a blackbird's
mournful sigh?

X.
Your urn is a cauldron,
an icy crucible, a house
for soft bones.

XI.
When I look in the mirror,

you stand behind me, your mouth
a black beak, your hand a talon resting
on the cusp of my shoulder.

XII.
I am never without you, blank
girl risen, witch-girl rising–
your spell follows me
through a crazed labyrinth
bent like a crooked spine.

XIII.
A woman
and a witch
are one.
A woman
and a witch
and a blackbird
are one.

Origin

The moon was risen, and by her light he discerned at some distance before him a number of the sea-people, who were dancing with great vigor on the smooth sand —The Mermaid Wife by Thomas Keightley

I am born in the swell of a blood-tide,
its rising groan carries me on supple

fingertips toward the plump yawn
of an inverted spiral, plummets

me southward, my earth an unearthing,
a dawn of muddied sky. Her sea-breath

greets my new form, balanced on the tip
of a wave, my birth a casual detour

from the moon's assessment. A shape-
shifter, the sea my burst chrysalis, awake

to the gentle curve of lithe shadows
following me across depths. *Follow me*

to this end–she spits me forth, another seal-
girl bent at the hip, reposed as if sleeping

on sand grains forming constellating
patterns of forgotten stars erased by time

& exposure. This is a song I've always
Known—I curl against myself like a nautilus

shell, my head filled with the sound
of broken waves. From far away,

she calls me back in a voice of rain,
singing *alone, alone, alone.*

PART TWO
POISONED APPLE

I desire the things which will destroy me in the end
—Sylvia Plath

Magdalene

And the twelve were with him, and also some women who had been healed of evil spirits and infirmities: Mary called Magdalene, from whom seven demons had gone out (Luke 8:1-2)

Version 1
Her repentant knees scrape a bed of sand.
She clasps the ache of a cross she has yet to bear.

Revision 2
She tosses a smile over her shoulder while the holy beg at her feet.

Revision 3
Her long hair curtains the shame painted across her cheeks.
    Her long hair curtains mirrors.
    Her long hair curtains feet as
    she anoints them with tendrils & kisses–

Revision 4
She is not the anointer, but the anointed.
    She cries ANOINT ME and men
    sign the cross across their throats.

Revision 5
Her life is sand

that flutters quick and nervous as a butterfly's wings,
then eats its mouth dry.
An hourglass meeting its reversal
time and time again.

Revision 6
Seven demons. Not an exorcism
    but a homecoming. They, trusty
    gargoyles, find shelter in her deep caves.

Revision 7
Tête-à-tête with the other Marys,
    they roll their eyes to the heavens,
    holding laughing skulls.

Revision 8
There is love, she knows it
    when her thighs collect
    the dew of holy water.

Revision 9
Witness, she must bear this apple
    of knowledge, this x of
    indignation and thorns
    even as she cries his return.

Revision 10
Now, she does not
    fall to her knees, repentance

>is not an even exchange for
>pleasure. Instead–

Revision II
She slips a skull
>into her pocket,
>gathers her Marys
>and rides the even keel
>of a ship toward the
>blue yawn of a waiting sun.

Prayer for a Witch

Christ,

    she has been found   plucking blackberries

from her stomach, swallowing   berries whole

    without dismay, with fervor, with

        longing. She has been

found gestating damp daydreams.   She has

    lips smothered in   detritus, save

her, O Lord, from fondling   rough bark & cats'

    eyes & blank thighs   she has been found

plump in solitude, whistling amongst   feathers, gathering

    her openness, splayed belief   rising, her body

an open tomb   Christ, she has been   found enjoying

    the frock of sunrise   the sound of glass   breaking, the sadness

of a bell, the way our collected hurts   stick to her like

whispers. Christ, remove her   from this swollen world,   remove

    her & the like from this–

remove

    her.

Shannon Kearns

Night Out

by night,
I paint
my face with

pretty. Lick
gloss, eyeless
pout. liner, black

and thick
to fake
desire. tsunamis
pour endless
founts of

courage
from thin-
necked
bottles.

    there are boys:
    their smiles
    tiny gold stars,
    their pyrite hands
    mystic rectangles–

I want their love
like I wanted to be
cradled by the woman
who made me then returned
to her constellation. In the

end, there's nothing
but a split||wound between
her legs and mine where
loss festers a putrid lotus–

        maybe it's
        because my
        dress||seam

        ripped open on
        the way here,
        or how I'm wearing
        my mother's shoes,
        but tonight I want

        nothing but a crown
        of fingers coronating
        my throat. nothing but

        a mother waking
        in the middle
        of the night wondering
        if I'm her gasping

        daughter.

Yellow

Now why should that man have fainted? But he did, and right across my path by the wall, so that I had to creep over him every time!
 —Charlotte Perkins Gilman, *The Yellow Wallpaper*

    Speaking of hyster-
ics [I thought they'd get your attention]
    once, you undid my nightgown revealing
a crescent moon, a vertical smile [waning]
    toward dark. As you spread me flat

and tucked in my corners, I counted the men
    who've sewn themselves a comfortable home
in my belly [house of thread]
    alternating stitches, deciding
[with care] exactly how tight to

    tie off the thread. Didn't I say
they tuck themselves in at night [whispering]
    under a yellow roof about how
funny I am [I don't even know they're there!]

    Speaking of yellow, I've tried
finding a corner of sunlight [to peel back]
    blackness. Isn't it funny how
I can see [what you can't?]

I'll admit, it can be hard to find me [in the dark.]
Men want to paint my body from the inside. Can't stand
    a face without a smile [*won't you smile for me, girl?*]
Run their hands like mustard river water across
    my bars, licking their teeth, thinking of how deeply

they can bury themselves in my belly, how long they can [stay]
    without my noticing. But, I tell you, I do notice:
yellow eye, wolf eye, sees through the dark. And I see them,
    all the same, all hungry for some mother [love]. So,

the story goes [always the same] I pull them like rabbits
    [from a burrow] and toss them, crying
yellow, into the waiting mouth of a bear.

Lotus Eater

Brooklyn, you were a hot mouth of wolf-
hunger. Those nights, you ate me whole,

ribs & everything, then spit out
an acid sunrise–orange

blisters split and cackling, or maybe
it was you pouring laughter, filthy

and bright. I forgot everything
but the cross painted on your right arm,

your faceless cathedral. I blessed
it as sirens stormed daylight

through open windows. I forgot
the black coffin of the 7 train and

the sweet, dank stench of subway breath
imparted tenderly from its glowing innards.

Those nights, I wanted and I
wanted and I wanted

your city heat and its grave undoing. Tell me
you wanted me, too—pink and lonesome, melted

into your cloistered grip. Tell me you wanted
my body strewn across your floor, soft and broken.

My Body is a Church

I have built myself into   the architecture

                    of this house   its bones   ache

          silent messages scribe   in tiny   imploding   dream

worlds that   visit me while I   lay blankly   in a bed of scripture–

      how many words   have I inhaled   because of you?   My body

is nailed   to the *t*   of trans *fix* ation,   trans *form* ation

            but always a cost, accosted while I sleep by remnants

of a forlorn church   its pews   slice rows of petulance with bobbing

        gray heads nodding yes and, oh   how I want

            to say yes   not to a god   or the many gods I have

      placed   on my altar (god of shame, god of good, god of nothing)

how I want   to say   yes   to a garden

        of spindly yearnings   that desiccate   the architecture

            of that good   and that god   and grow like ivy cracking

      marrow–   it happens this time   each year

my dreams turn toward   death chiming   while I kneel

        in the shadow   of my own spell   casting stones at stained-

glass windows as   my eyes, too,   shatter and blind

48   *The Uterus is an Impossible Forest*

The Burning

There is a diary and in that diary the word SHAME eats bare
lines with pink capital letters shaped like knives. The diary claims
        to know nothing. It will not speak, even if spoken to. It will not
touch, or defy, or instigate. It knows how to keep a secret,
        even as its white, tender pages are mutilated.

There is a girl and in that girl hides a bear eating her shame,
        licking its paws clean of fury. It stalks her dreams, silent-footed, open-
mouthed, searching for a way in. There is always a bear and it is always
hungry. The girl, she has forgotten how to pray, but she knows the end
        of this dream. Always the same–the bear kneels before her, raises its head
to a bear-god, and stretches its jaws in an invitation–   *follow me.*

I am looking at a bush. All summer, it has been silent. Yes, it sprouted
        green leaves, yet I wondered, is this a weed? Should I cut it? Should I
dig it up and burn its roots? Should I let it grow? Now, one flower
        has emerged, and it is pink and pointed toward the sun. It needed some time,
it didn't know what it was or could be.

    All summer, I have been burning. There is a girl, and in that girl is one flower. I watch her tilt the arch of her neck

        toward my golden fire and there is an ache, but there is a bear

and a blank page and a pink pen shaped like a cliff,

        shaped like an ending, and if I write one more word

or dream one more dream, or touch her one more time,

        I will have to rip myself from where I've been planted,

year after year, burn my roots, turn toward the bear and cry   *Bite!*

Lilith

I tried to tell him:
    unfurling is becoming of me.
    He didn't want to look
    at the yawn, preferring to pluck
    and plant me in the midst of a godless bloom.

I could not avoid: spreading this seed,
    lily that I am. Lily that I am, stamen and pistil
    are mine, an ineffable daydream. Yes, he made me lie
    beneath his sovereign weight, trinket that I was, plaything that I was.

No more: this land a woman's,
    this land my heave, like breasts, water
    of milk tinged with the yellow of a waiting sun that begs
    me for permission to leave each day. These hours are mine. These hours

have forged me a crown of teeth
    and a pair of wings. Crouching on a dirt throne,
    I will call out the words of everything he's tried
    to hold and found too wild&bony&rough for his taste.

I tell him: write my name.
I tell him: cast my name upon gold.

Remember my capable hands:
    I will hold soil because soil is not a thing
    you can own. I am not a thing
    you can own. Lay me across a rushing
    river, and I will be a bridge, but never

will I stand, lily in your garden,
a mirror for your stone gaze.

Body, Undone

Madness is a fat sapphire, dauntless
    and craving. Trace the spirals
of my form searching
    for desires, elegant & tucked
in belly folds, each soft roll hiding
    another love letter, another master. Madness is
a fragile neck, swan's bridge, seat of
    language, of *utter,* words of deep and utter
trial, held fast, made slow, made to pour
    open-tongued into steaming
cauldrons. They command EAT
    and I swallow their curd. I grow tender. I grow
children and sacrifices. They command
    STOP and my body becomes a forgotten cistern: hot
dry, and buried. Madness is a forgotten woman. Madness is
    a command. They cry
SPEAK: my urge is not enough. They cry
    SPEAK: my repentance is not enough–

Dream Inside of a Glass House

Windows upon windows. I am a spectacle. Please knock before you enter. I will see you coming long before you arrive. Greetings, I am a cannibal on display. I devour bodies for a living. My pleasure is the salt of your residue. Greetings, you have found me asking for my shame to be revealed like a slice of white thigh. Call me what you will– your stones are merely echoes of my moans. The cracks in my glass are fault lines in my palms calling in a future where transparent walls are unspoken invitations, a dinner bell for a feast.

Mad Woman

i.
Bloom of dark incoherence,
this ~~madness~~ only a slight detour

from a fated night sky, its blinding
stars white ~~rage~~. I meet you

in the clearing of a forest, the earth
soft and supple as the spill

of an ~~open wound~~. Blackness grows
thick in this place. ~~Hush~~, the branches

scratch whispers in silent
air. I am alone, my scent putrid

as a caged beast stalking silver
shadows. ~~Hunger~~ prowls

my spine with gnarled fingertips,
a dizzy reminder of eternal

~~emptiness~~. I might try to forget
the gnawing bone of ~~desire~~

lodged in my throat. I might try
to purge my ~~rage~~ into a nest of moss,

soft as a mother, let it hold the gnarled
teeth of the other body, the ~~secret~~ one

that lives on the other side of everything
I cannot say. I will fall to my knees ~~begging~~

for another story–one where the woman
in the tower does not ~~mistake~~ her ceiling for the sky.

ii.
~~Blind~~ madness ~~follows~~
~~me into the eye of my rage,~~

~~haunted as an~~ open wound,
~~the blood a swift~~ hush

~~silencing~~ hunger
~~to~~ emptiness. Desire,

~~a longing so~~ secret, ~~so~~
~~tamed, I find my body~~

~~on all fours~~ begging
~~to be released from~~
~~my~~ mistake.

Woman as Yes

This voice, my voice,
my words originating
in a melted birth-
place. This voice,
my voice, a woman's
voice always saying
yes like a wind instrument,
breathy and high-pitched
to impart niceties and polite
meanderings of conversation,
mellow as a daisy field. *Yes,*
like a flicker, snuffed not
satisfied, offered in a jeweled
box lined with velvet folds–
a body in a box. A *yes* to
be touched and pulled and
smothered. I have spun my
yes into yarn, wrapped a
web around my mouth, wrapped
a web around my throat, cradled
my unspoken words in my mouth,
dry and dense. I have been
taught my *yes* is a tamed wind,
don't let it topple.
I have given *yes* over

and over until all that's left
is a hollow egg,
brittle and bearing.

Woman as Artificial [Intelligence]

After Barbara Zucker's sculpture series *For Beauty's Sake*

    [Hold your applause]   I am   a woman

ready to be   seen,   I   am a   woman,

      silken   untied   applied   severed

              from   my   animal   parts

screwed   together   in   formations

      arousing   prescribed   pleasure   [Hold

          your   applause]   I

am   a   (woe)man   perfect && redeemed

Skin

On returning to the shore, he met the fairest maiden that eye ever gazed upon: she was walking backwards and forwards, lamenting in most piteous tones the loss of her seal-skin robe —The Mermaid Wife by Thomas Keightley

In the darkness of a lost truth, my un-cloaked figure
lies naked of its rights. I have been swallowed
by sharp edges & limbs, a place of gravity
thick as a drowned bell echoing a cry for *home*

She meets me where water kisses sky kisses sand,
her wet mouth a lopsided smile, eerie as a black,
underwater cave lurking in blended ocean corners,
somewhere between here and there, & I,
I am taken. She holds my skin, crumpled rainbow
of sleek fur & lichen-studded bliss, her fingernails
shaped like teeth tearing a land song

into my woven tempest. We face each other,
my face damp with prismatic visions
of a future-self beholden to a body
only half mine. The sky is a prophecy:
a forlorn gull scrapes her wing
against a veiled mist–bride

of fog & wind, bride of skin peeled

& hidden behind latches. Her skeleton
key catches a nervous breeze

and buries itself in garden loam, & I
am nothing but a locked door.

PART THREE
MOTHER WOLF

In my hunger,
every little voice

could have been
a daughter

—Claire Wahmanholm, "Hunger" from *Meltwater*

Habits

(I repeat)

      my knife is sharpened

  by the raw edge

of this mountain, and it digs

     into the soft part of

  my back when

I keep it pocketed.

(I repeat)

      my knife is an instrument

  of decay. I use it

to decimate apples

     into tiny, bite-size

  pieces only to be distributed

into the compost of your body.

(I repeat)

     dinner is served

  on a neat table

and I've swept the crumbs

     and resulting refuse

  into the sadness

of a black can.

(I repeat)

                my knife is a carver

        of wood, and apples, and

time. It knows my habits,

              the way I like to be held,

    the way I turn toward its

precious heaviness.

(I repeat)

           you've asked and asked,

    and I've relented. Yes–

my knife is a mother, you may

              see her teeth, run your fingers along her spine,

    take pleasure in her heft as you run her smoothly

through the ripeness of late summer flesh.

Postpartum

Child, I've heard your owl cry, but it seeps wastefully   in my bones. Hollow

    stare of pines, do you know   winter as I do? Are your bitter needles

a carpet, a bed to sleep upon, or a tea to brew   to assuage me of my guilt? Bare

    trees, you try my patience with your   vacancies. I   cannot bear

    your unabashed nakedness, your dormant vigor.   How do I

respond to the thrash and moan   of your branches when my winter is so thick?

    I will deny your invitation to find you beautiful.   I will hold my own

hand in the night, even when there are cries,   even when, Child, I cannot

find your light—

Broken Waters

This bath, an ocean of maladies, rich with matter and memory. You, a floating precipice, your edge a break in clouds calling thunderous light, a herald, a black flag. I suppose these waters must drown and fill and drown and fill before I can know their depths.

I grew you an ocean–if I could merely float with you, perhaps I wouldn't find myself caught in blue terror. Before I face the opening of this drain, something else inside me might spill forth in raucous melodies like *gash* or *depart* or *sob*.

Will you estrange me now, at this final moment? you, attached with your tender malignancies? you, whom I've cradled in this split? I cannot bear the rush, your surrender. I've waited for this moment and prayed for

unclenching, yet when it comes,
I have nothing in me but screams.

Alchemical Reaction

Those were the haunting days of early May, every daffodil wilted like a dying child. My bones were not bones but snapped twigs. The light was a crescendo, high-pitched then fading. Everything appeared still in its brilliance. Each night I dreamt of swans in flight. Each morning my breasts cried for release. We took turns watching you breathe. I became an apparition, pained and faded, eating promises, shedding hope. I became my own experiment, a hypothesis in survival: how much more before ironclad madness? How much more before gold? You slept in a glass box, boy on a shelf. I was told to call if your lips turned blue, blue as a May sky, blue as a mistake. Those were the waiting days of hunger and solitude, transmuted and forlorn.

When my body bleeds, I dream of spirals

My bed curves   bright dreams   in labyrinthine consequences, driving starlight   into pools   at the lips   of my scars. Infinite   shapes elaborate   upon the   water of rust & drainage   running   like a cut   along the soft   inner world   of circuitous   faults. My children were born   just in time.   My body   remembers   their arrival   each month, & opens its   gates to reveal   the kiss   of red love,   both un-   knowable and known,   like a hand drawing   spirals on   a white page

Domestic Silence

I.   A woman sits
           at a window,

      wraps her hand
           around her mouth, stifling

      the birth of a sob.
           She has learned

      her silence
           is a suture.

II.   Red daydreams
           creep through door

      jambs, linger
           around the edges

      of her eyes. She wipes
           them clean

      with a white cloth
           stained crimson.

III. Her child is a crow.
   It eats from the flesh

 of her palm.
   Only the crow

 is allowed to cry.
   The woman watches

 its long, black beak open
   and release

 a satisfied *caw*
   that rattles like a fist-

 full of pebbles in her
   empty chest.

IV. The house has grown
   cold. Her body

 is a specter, spectator
   of dust's dance,

 cracked light bulbs,
   & the lick of accumulated

 grime at the edges
   of everything.

V. Perhaps she should light
        a match for warmth,

twirl smoke lazily
        around her finger-

tips, draw a dream
        in thin air,

blow out the match,
        make a wish,

make a promise
        not to tell—

Hornet's Nest

I never wanted a paper house,
house of bitter, house of chewed

trees & spit where everything
can burn. Isn't fire just another

word for the end? Nothing here
is written, everything blends into pulp.

                        I cannot separate
                          he pieces into piles—what is wood

                          and what is wet? Where is
                          the salivating beast

building her trap? She utters a curdling
buzz turning milk into a yellowed

fever flush, turning a nipple into
a vortex, paroxysm of flesh.

                     And I am her, I am here sticky as a sin, gathering
                     gray shards, carefully wrapping each around

my eyes, my nose, my mouth
until I cannot find a way out.

i dream my body splits in two

round body draped, heaving choke facedown in a pillow, fake velvet molded mask, lips a low
O of open & often & overflow. ripe, i spit hard cherry stones at an invisible
mother, let the rich juice drip bloody lines down my chin, the red flesh just another latent
longing. a siren sings pain's ghost to slumber   & i stumble through hallways littered
with time's constant ache–crumpled doctor's slips, a dry, white plastic stick, its cross a covenant.
       O, i am
opening like sight lines in a painting, the way my eye is drawn from left to right to corners to
ceilings, movement akin to a midwife's firm grasp,   knees wide as beating wings *up
down in out left right left*   & i am hearing the call of an ancient becoming, portal to
land, solid, firm. i am a tunnel, a corridor from unknown to known, a purged deliverance– O

Nine Months

i. I pluck a strand of hair, twist it into a snake
    & bake it into the tender innards of a pie.

ii. A bird lands on the nape of my window, shuffles
    blue wings then drops a feather, its plume an oracle.
    I trace my lips with its tip, flick the crest of my belly
    with the memory of flight.

iii. Nothing dies here, but I am convinced otherwise. I search
    the white paper for a speck of blood. It is fall and the air
    smells like leaving.

iv. I dream of mothers. Every night they visit me with their mouths
    open, spawning silent words. I wonder if they are mirrors or
    windows or ancestors, grave and warning. I dream of a forest
    with a path and a sign: *not this way*

v. What is new life if, in its blessed awakening, it burns everything
    in its wake? My body is a coffin. My body is a burial. My spine
    is a broom handle. I sweep my ashes into soft mounds.

vi. *Listen* A mother's hum is but a dirge. She cradles notes on her tongue
    then swallows them whole. *Listen* She has sung herself to sleep.

vii. January's gray is a blank stare. I decorate a room with fragments of light. A rocking chair is placed across from a window. Someday, my future self will reach through the veil of a dream to visit this chair where a woman died and a baby found life, again & again.

viii. I am not a mirror, I am a mask. I dam the torrent of my body and tuck my ocean into a crib.

ix. Baby, baby A completion. A cold cup of tea. Silent trees. My breasts leak tears. *Baby, baby* A muddle of blankets. Dried blood. A sharp bite. Separate. Separating like a fallen tooth. *Baby, baby* A scent of sea. La mer. La mère. Salt and water, stirred, dissolve into one.

My breasts leak soft tears

After *Let-Down* by Loie Holowell

In the aftermath, my body is a broken
urn, blackened rim faded gray, opening
toward a stream where two eyes unfold
a yellow grin–Here are the other eyes,
the watching ones that seek a supple
form. An apple, bruised and skinned,
its raw flesh craving the bite. All day
I have cradled this need in my palm.
All day my body has churned toward
this need–a mouth incessant, a tongue
coated white like the belly of a dove.
        There is a house at the edge of my mind.
        It calls to me in the darkest hours, the time
        when I cup my hand around the velvet
        dome of a baby's head. When I cup my hand
        around the swell of my lips and our cries mingle
        as one sound. There is a house at the edge
        of my curled fingers, close enough to touch,
        where my body knows the cedar scent of its
        strong eaves and the cradle in the corner
        grows a ravenous bouquet of wildflowers.

Mastitis

not the heat   not the cup of breast

    not the lineation [striation] of turn signals

        on sediment, rock, stone

located to the left of softness. block, you are

        the staunching of my river–

the dam of my 2 am delirium. you, the inflation, the

        collapse, you the culprit in my

fever dream, body fighting the miniscule, body fighting–

        block, you are the aftermath

of my nestled daydreams. I massage your sand-spit tenderly

        with glass fingertips hoping for the

breaking, the breaking–

House

House you are a stone
embrace at the center

of my reckoning.
Children haunt your corners,

echoing pale laughter.
Nothing grows here

but our bodies and
your roses. You, house

of constellating fissures,
you know your center–

goddess' iris,
queen bee's hive dance,

mother-tongue,
can you show me mine?

Make me a descendant
of your ruins, build me

a narrow staircase
and watch me navigate

my ascension toward
your crystal eye?

Waxing Moon

I rock you to sleep under my monster eye,
lids curved like the crescent of a waxing
moon, the sliver of my iris a warning–
fatigue is the food of a fever dream.

Sweet child, do you know your mother
is a mirror? Behind the glass I lay in wait,
my jaws, a snap of memory. My hands, two
luminaries holding judgment and faith–
neither have a voice.

Show me the real mother, the one
who tucks blankets & measures
medicine & slips behind her own eyes
when the waxing moon becomes too bright.

Show me the real mother and I'll find myself
behind her reflection, my eyes aglow in the shadow
of her darkness, my mouth the shape of a howl.

i dream my body is a grave

Under the thick loam of dark earth, I have buried my body. It is tender

in its demise, a pale flower. A smile blooms white on its lips. A snake

is wrapped around its neck hissing green silence. Everything is still.

Everything is curtained. My body has forgotten its weight.

My body is waiting for a sign. I gaze into the mouth

of its grave, a gorgeous swallow, a gulp of ashes.

Nothing can touch me except time. Sweet, dank soil, wrap

me in the arms of your decay. Melt me into your belly, your roots the

tug of an umbilical cord, your wet twilight, a heavy uterus,

ready for the purge of blood, sick river, thick with sorrow.

i bleed red dreams

into the rectory of my body. A baby was housed
here, limbs curled into spirals, teeth a dormant fence.

Mother was the word it spoke in circles, etching walls
of muscle and bone with the name of the banshee,

Cyhyraeth, wraith/woman wailing into the blank faces of trees.
Her long hair presides over the cliffs of her shoulders, her spine

my walking stick leading me over the edge of my own
dark woods. Her mouth, the split wound residing

in my belly. Her lips part to reveal a crooked
staircase and I descend, her tongue a sharp object

cutting stars into the notches of my feet. Her voice
the rain of blood washing my body in slow circles,

pulling me into a red fog, her breath a mourning song–
[hair/spine/mouth/lips/tongue/voice the rain/breath]

the soft bowl of my uterus purging

the motherbodies/the forgotten.

Visitations

Maiden

Just beginning
to know the
commandment of
my hips, to
notice the moon
of my body
waxing toward fullness,
the way
its bright desire
stirs cauldrons.

I am a reflection,
sixteen and standing
in my bathroom mirror
tracing the growing
sway of circles

that seek my
attention. I am
learning how I
can be desired
without feeling,

anything, how to ride on the wing-

tip of a feral dawn, blowing
ripples & kisses & knowing
beauty is a coin.

It is then
the witch arrives
on my doorstep,
crosses my threshold,
wraps me in her
spring, an early

awakening that expects
nothing and is surprised
by its own flourishing.

The orb of an apple
appears in the
nightshade folds of her
voluminous cloak.

She commands   *eat*

then chuckles, hissing

                 not a maiden

as she watches
my neck bow
to the taste
of its flesh.

Mother

Glancing around my house,
she looks away
from the accumulation
of my discarded desires
collected in rambling corners.
A baby's cry rattles her,
and I remember my own
vast spring. She moves like
wind toward the cradle, clasping
a dandelion plucked from the fields
of her emerald cloak. Her lips
part, a crucible. Tilting forward,
she spills hot breath over its
fragile spores, spreading them
like a promise across the baby's
cheeks. Rising, she gathers my
limbs and arranges them like
branches, tucking them softly
around my tender trunk.
She lays me prone on her cloak,
bed of grass, as I germinate
the stars of seeds in soil.

Crone

We sit together, counting
our days, a pebble for each.
They are numerous, held
fast in our cracked wishes.

We are the same, you & I
I whisper. She nods, pulls
a green ribbon from her cloak,
ties it jauntily around her neck
as if to say, *see, I can be carefree.*

There's nothing here but a crow
perched on a lamppost outside our
door. We've been forgotten by all
but birds. No matter, we have pie
and a song we keep forgetting.

I'll set the table with
pearl-handled utensils and she'll
carve chairs from the bones
of those we've loved.

Sea-Hag

They were married, and lived together for many years, during which time they had several children, who retained no vestiges of their marine origin, saving a thin web between their fingers, and a bend of their hands, resembling that of the fore paws of a seal
—The Mermaid Wife by Thomas Keightley

My children   are tumbled shards   of sea-glass.

       I collect them at the tide's edge   against the howl

of a mourning wind.   Their bodies clink   soft   daydreams

     of the places   they roamed before   the before.

       Their eyes are   mine, translucent   opal sheen,

their webbed skin   smells of Her.   I rinse them

clean   in her waters,   water of my

     bone-change,   rubbing their bellies   with a pulsing

ebb.   Ever tender, I long   to take each sliver   of ocean-birth

     in my mouth,   nestle them under   my tongue, roll

       their cries   into the silence   of my clenched teeth

then swallow hard–my throat   a shadow, my belly   a writhing calamity.

PART FOUR
RETURN

This is the year of scraping out hauntings.
I said no. Now I shove that ghost into the fold,
Press back, iron the sheets of my choosing

—Simone Muench & Jackie K. White, "Pressed"
from *Hex & Howl*

Protection

Dark angel, you are   the shadow   lingering   in the corners

     of *never*.   Empty soul, I'm wed   to a ghost.

Alone, I live   my ring   a silenced

     noose, a throttling,   a hand   wrapped

quietly around my   throat,   fingers carved   like

     tree lines. How many   years   have I lived   hiding

in the hollow   of sick woods?   Dark   angel,

     I speak these   words   with you–

     Bone   *Obsidian*   *Hematite Cast*   *Merkaba*   *Metatron*

     A fortress   A fortress

A gallows

     Oblivion   *Remember*   *Rise*

Sever

Hecate

I am a full goblet,
empty plate,
shard of bone.

My cave dwells
under the dearth
of a severed moon.

I am the face you
see at the end
when choice is a knife

carving divergent lines
into the trunk of a patient
tree. I collect its sap,

mix it with my blood,
feed it to the roots,
calling on protection

from the stones
embedded in my
crown. I foretell

your future: a baby
without a name.
darkness in the under-

belly of the year.
An underworld
to call home.

I will hold all
you are called
to forget, all

you are called
to regret, in
the cradle of my hand.

White Gardenias

This, an elegy for desire,
unstemmed from white

flower, petals a hushed
plea. I am nothing

but a bee wandering
in place, each flower

a missive written
in honey, parched by

a distant fuse, its burning
unsung and holy. I am

nothing but a fence–
iron lace secluding

the rampant thirst
of untended blooms,

delicate as a finger, cut
and arranged in glass

Once again, I find myself on the other side of my tomb

Out of the ash
I rise with my red hair
And I eat men like air.
—"Lady Lazarus" by Sylvia Plath

    There is a woman beside me and her hair smells of fire. She keeps

dropping ashes into her coffee and stirring them with the tip

    of her ring finger. A door is cut into the softness of our room. Always,

she paints the edges black and stamps them with her mouth,

    as if to say *yes*. As if to say, *death*. The shadow of her fingers

on my palm. My tomb is a room where I empty my burdens: diamonds & china &

    framed pictures depicting a face I thought was mine. (It was simply

the silhouette of a body I used to own). She has a talent for knowing

    the shape of memories and transforming them into spells. I watch her

make a sigil from consonants, place it in a jar, cover it with snake-

    skin & cinnamon & copper dust & Florida

water then smile at me as if to say, *See, happiness can be easy*. As if

    to say, *See, death becomes you*.

Pyre

You whisper into the mouth of a teacup, draining the last of its silver with the clamp of your lips. Your fingers are tangled in the breath of a fog borne from the way your hair clings to your damp neck. Your tongue is only the space between our words. There is a child in the corner of your house. She sings your sadness in splintered notes. I gather the pieces, careful not to prick my fingers. Her body looks like yours, but thinner, as if disappearance were her ritual. I imagine her bundling sage and hawthorn into the pucker of her lap, counting their buds one by one into the length of a funeral pyre. I imagine her laying your body lightly on the wooden bed, so fragrant, so flammable. She would stroke one nail down the line of your breasts, your stomach, tracing your organs, gripping flesh, licking bones, licking fire set so carefully in the small pool of your back. She'd lay a quilt across your face and sing you to sleep, her voice casting soft fortunes into the ravenous flames.

Scarecrow

There was a body & for a while, I thought   it was mine. It wept slivers of iron madness, sunk
in black rows   I arranged &   positioned for proper burial. There was a body &
it was his. I carried it dutifully to its funeral pose, a hand   raised in greeting
to the crows who gathered round, black as a widow's   dress. I pulled their wings
tightly around my throat. There was a body and I stripped it clean, replaced its flesh
with dry straw, carefully
buttoned a brown, flannel shirt across its   empty chest, caressed its
amputated   hands with the twist of a knot. I painted a smile on
his sock face & wrote my name across his   eyes. On harvest nights I gather what
remains   of his bones, picked clean, tie them to the mouth of a chime, and listen
to the echo of his body beat against moonlight. There was a body & in the end,
it was mine.

Door

I'm always trying to paint that door—I never quite get it
—Georgia O'Keeffe on her painting *In the Patio No. IV*

Bronzed threshold holding sorry mutations of my form begging forgiveness for standing on the wrong side of closed. Precious knob, excise my worsted guilt spun behind tears, wetting knots, teasing all that's been tied apart. I did not know this door, its solid pine opacity, would lend itself dutifully to decimation. My nails scratch at weakened hinges, always catching a thread on red-rusted joints, *always* unraveling all that's been taut. *I've never quite gotten* a glimpse past, only a sliver, thin as a needle, pipes lucid notes into the shadows of my self-loathing. Door– *I'm trying* *to get it right* this time, this time I'll paint you black & cover my teeth marks engraved on the curve of your lock, pretend I've known your secret all along.

Sister-Self

Dearest {Sister-Self},

    Mother grew us like an afterthought. We exist
in the form of {one} body {or forest} –
My body has {always} been a poem I cannot remember
I have forgotten all I was meant to be {come} {a cry}
from beyond the wall of trees {Sister} you are a blackened
limb I have tucked behind {my back} In your fire dance
of ash & curdling tears, I am becoming {you}{again}

    Nothing of me remains but a fence of skin stretched
like lace at the edge of wild {Sister} you know
the way through these woods and what sly tangles
they {hold} Draw me a map back to the clearing
where our shared forest sighs open–

    {Shadow-sister}with hair of fallen leaves, may I bury
my face into the arm, damp earth of your neck
& allow the swallow of your body to carry me toward

    {my return}

Rebirth

Under the thick loam of dark earth, I have buried   my body. It is tender

in its demise,   a pale flower. A smile blooms white on its lips.   A snake

is wrapped around its neck   hissing green silence.   Everything is still.

    Everything is curtained.   My body has forgotten   its weight.

My body is   waiting   for a sign.   I gaze into the mouth

    of its grave, a gorgeous   swallow, a gulp of ashes.

    Nothing can touch me   except time. Sweet, dank soil,   wrap

me in the arms   of your decay.   Melt me into your belly,   your roots the

    tug of an umbilical cord,   your wet twilight a heavy uterus,

ready for the purge   of blood, sick   river, thick with sorrow.

Love Letter to a Witch

Magic girl,   I bow   to your spell,

     your incantation   parts wild   seas. Flower-

essence   vapor-breath   rides midnight

     to a moon   swaying   bright against black.

Tell me,   do the woods   know your name?

     Do the ash   trees   follow the wind   of your calling,

ebbing with   each lilting   note?   I have tried

to follow you   into thickets   dense with shadow

     & found   your dance   both riveting

        & impossible.   Tell me,   do you emulate

the gyre of a falcon   or the rush   of a brook?   Magic

     girl, I want   to know the secret   of your dandelion

storm. Fade me   into the puff-cloud   of your wish & I'll float

     trapped in your breeze   into the dark soil   of my new belonging.

Crow

In the dream, my kitchen is beautiful. The floors are rich terra-cotta, the light is not light but soft black, the black of Prospero's magic. My desires are being cooked in pots. Steam rises, braiding nostalgic lust with future longings, fragrant hunger. There is a window, my mother's window, looking out to a backyard redolent with cardinals, red as tongues.

You're there, standing at the window. Light filters around your black form. Your shadow is full of thought. I wear your aura like a cloak. Your hair is long, it brushes the back of your neck like feathers. Turning, I see you faceless and full of flight. The kitchen becomes

stairs, becomes a bedroom balanced at the top. All paths lead here. All paths lead to this–me dark and wanting, you a bridge, a bent wing.

Orchid

Everything in this room is sacred, everything in this room belongs to us. There is a heavy door & a key embedded with pearls. I tuck our secrets between my breasts. I string memories of velvet around the open arms of a crystal chandelier. She greets me on the other side of forever, her bounty a candle's flickering tongue. Her arms are two white ribbons, her legs, two orchid stems. We anoint the walls with the lace of our sighs. I have painted my reflection on the window. It watches me without shame. My eyes meet my eyes meet two irises aglow, red as apples, reflecting the curve of a nascent flame risen from silk touching silk touching bone–

Spun

A mother, a mother, a Mary.
A baby, a body, a child.
A knot, a knot, a jellybean.
A belly, a mammary, a memory.

I am a cottage in her magenta forest.
She crouches in the shadows of trees,
hums with bumblebees, collects fairies
under my eaves. Climbs into a pile of dreams.

Lay beside me, her hands
are mine, long fingered and slender,
pale pine needles. Our words, a coiled skein.

Daughter, for how long? The edge,
the edge, a baby, a body already
budding. The child already
rotting. *Lay beside me—tell me*

about the day I was born. A baby,
a body, a mother, a Mary. A knot,
a knot. Daughter, how long
before the spinning wheel's
click turns you into a clock?

Hair

For Emma

I spend daylight untangling knots from my daughter's hair. Her face is a disappearing act behind the crown of her yellow cascade snarled like yarn in a storm between her eyebrows, her eyes a blue, melted forest. Bones of her shoulders small boulders rounded against the ominous swish of the comb's sharp teeth. I wonder at the patina of her skin, the way it covers the tiny rivers of her soft oblivion, smooth as a nautilus, a mask she hasn't learned to wear. Her peach head turned to smooth blonde turned to waist-length wanderings, each tendril a secret snaking its way inward toward her smokescreen cave. An invitation is needed to enter, and I know, the space will only grow. One day, I'll knock at her entrance and wait for permission to enter beyond her dense veil.

Return

Thus glided away years, and her hopes of leaving the upper world had nearly vanished, when it chanced one day, that one of the children, playing behind a stack of corn, found a seal-skin...One thing alone was a drawback on her raptures. She loved her children, and she was now about to leave them for ever —The Mermaid Wife by Thomas Keightley

Child, you are a blue discovery, last note of a distant song.
    Your small hands have located my trust. I bend to your blessing:
my skin–lost mother, lost friend, lost self.
    You hold it to your chest; your gaze, an open door.

How do I claim it with you so near and tender? Must
    I swallow you wholly back into my belly
& carry you into the depths of my un-curtained belonging?
    Will this appetite of mine never cease?

I've been told to write my gratitudes in blood, make a blood
    pact to *stay, stay, stay*–All the while, my heart-tug
follows the moon's gravitational pull & I am pulled *away, away,*
    away–Child, how do I choose?

    An ocean or green laughter, an ocean
    or sweetdamp cheeks round as apples, an ocean or–

I wrap your still body carefully in my coat, enfold
    you in a wet, dark womb, these waters just another room in our house.
Goodbye is a sharp breath, a deep slit, as we slip
    sleekly into the heaving chest of a waiting mother.

Holding my child for the first time

This, a shadowing
This, a pull in thread
This, a tear of suppleness
This, a tear of milk-water
This, a dislodged membrane
This, a thrust of arms
This, a sky of complacent sunshine
This, a nibble, sharp and clean
This, a startling effigy
This, a clinging
This, a scent of burnt hair
This, white lace and curtains
This, a cave-mother
This, a recent expanse
This, a dread song
This, a licked envelope
This, a surfeit apology
This, a wolf's grin
This, a tender [terrifying] gateway
This, an impossible forest

Acknowledgments

I am so grateful for everyone who helped bring this collection to life. First, and foremost, Stephanie M. Wytovich believed in these words long before any of them were published. Thank you for bringing me to the edge of the dark forest, and then guiding me every step of the way through.

Thank you to Jennifer Barnes and Raw Dog Screaming Press for beautifully compiling these poems into a published book.

I would also like to thank Western Connecticut State University and the faculty of the MFA program in Creative and Professional Writing for their support and championing of burgeoning writers like myself.

My children, Colin and Emma, who are my whole heart and live in the pages of this book, thank you for teaching me what love is every day. Thank you to my partner, Tara Kearns, who is my informal "editor" and biggest cheerleader – I couldn't ask for anything more.

Previously Published
(under the name Shannon Marzella)

Alchemical Reaction, *Humana Obscura*, Forthcoming
Body, Undone, Eunoia Review, December 2023
Domestic Silence, *Coffin Bell*, October 2024
Habits, *Sky Island Journal*, July 2023
i dream my body splits in two, *Coffin Bell*, October 2024
Lotus Eater, *Stonecoast Review*, June 2023
Mad Woman, *Howl Anthology*, Black Spot Books, Forthcoming
Magdalene, *SPIRIT Anthology*, White Stag Publishing, December 2023
My Body is a Church, *Ghost City Review*, October 2023
My Breasts Leak Soft Tears, *Coffin Bell*, October 2024
Nervous Breakdown, *Mulberry Literary*, November 2024
Pyre, *The Solitude Diaries*, Forthcoming
Three Mothers, *Bloodlore Anthology*, White Stag Publishing, Forthcoming
Visitations, *SPIRIT Anthology*, White Stag Publishing, December 2023
Waxing Moon, *Howl Anthology*, Black Spot Books, Forthcoming
When my body bleeds, I dream of spirals, *Coffin Bell*, October 2024
Yellow, *Coffin Bell*, October 2024

About the Author

Shannon Kearns holds an MFA in Creative and Professional Writing with a concentration in poetry from Western Connecticut State University. *Girl in Shadows*, her young adult novel, was published by Nymeria Publishing in 2021. Her poetry has been published in several journals including *Sky Island Journal, Stonecoast Review,* and *Ghost City Review*. She also has poems in various anthologies such as White Stag Publishing's *Spirit* anthology, and Humana Obscura's *Blue* anthology. Her debut poetry collection, *The Uterus is an Impossible Forest*, is published with Raw Dog Screaming Press. You can connect with her on Instagram @shannon_mk_writer or through her website www.shannonmkearns.com.